GALE
CENGAGE Learning

Novels for Students, Volume 2

Copyright © 1997

Gale Research
835 Penobscot Building
645 Griswold St.
Detroit, Ml 48226-4094

ISBN 0-7876-1687-7
ISSN 1094-3552

Printed in the United States of America
10 9 8 7 6 5 4

Flowers for Algernon

Daniel Keyes

1966

Introduction

Originally published as a short story in 1958, *Flowers for Algernon* appeared as a full-length novel in 1966 and has remained a critical and popular success. The novel is told as a series of "Progress Reports" written by Charlie Gordon, a thirty-two-year-old man whose Intelligence Quotient (IQ) of 68 is tripled by an experimental surgical procedure. Unfortunately, the effects of the operation wear off after several months, and at the end of the novel Charlie is once more of subnormal intelligence. Although originally published as a work of science fiction—the short story won the World Science Fiction Convention's Hugo Award and the novel won the Nebula Award of the Science Fiction Writers of America—Daniel Keyes's story has achieved wide popularity outside the science fiction field. Much of the novel's power comes from Keyes's remarkable use of first-person point of view, as Charlie's entries move from semi-literacy to complex sophistication and back to semi-literacy. And the character of Charlie Gordon is a memorable portrait of alienation, of an individual who is at odds with his society and who struggles to have satisfactory relationships with others. The novel gained additional fame when its 1968 film version, *Charly*, earned Cliff Robertson an Academy Award as Best Actor for his portrayal of Charlie Gordon. Although some critics have found portions of the novel overly predictable or sentimental, Keyes's most famous work has continued to enjoy great popularity. Over thirty years after publication, *Flowers for Algernon* is still regarded with both respect and affection by readers within both the science fiction community and the public at large.

Author Biography

Daniel Keyes was born in Brooklyn, New York, on August 9, 1927. He was educated at Brooklyn College, where he received an A.B. degree in 1950. After graduation, Keyes worked briefly as an associate editor for the magazine *Marvel Science Fiction* while pursuing his own writing career; he later taught high school English in Brooklyn. In 1952 he married Aurea Georgina Vazquez, with whom he had three children. Keyes returned to Brooklyn College, received an A.M. degree in 1961, and went on to teach English on the university level, first at Wayne State University in Detroit, Michigan, and then at Ohio University, where in the 1970s he became Professor of English and director of the university's creative writing center.

Keyes was still teaching high school English when he first published the work that would make his reputation. The original short story version of "Flowers for Algernon" appeared in *The Magazine of Fantasy and Science Fiction* in 1959. After the story won the Hugo Award for best science fiction story of the year and was adapted as a television drama, Keyes expanded the story into a novel, published in 1966. The novel won the Nebula Award of the Science Fiction Writers of America (tying with Samuel R. Delany's *Babel-i7)* and was filmed in 1968 as *Charly.* The film was a notable success, earning Cliff Robertson an Academy

Award as Best Actor for his portrayal of Charlie Gordon.

Although none of Keyes' other work has achieved the popular and critical success of *Flowers for Algernon*, he has continued to write while pursuing a full-time career in English academics. He published two other novels, *The Touch* (1968) and *The Fifth Sally* (1980), and the nonfiction works *The Minds of Billy Milligan* (1981) and *Unveiling Claudia: A True Story of a Serial Murder* (1986). Both *The Minds of Billy Milligan* and *The Fifth Sally* share with *Flowers for Algernon* a concern with extraordinary psychological states, as both books examine the phenomenon of multiple personalities. Indeed, Keyes was able to write his book on Billy Milligan—the first person in the United States ever acquitted of a major felony on the grounds of multiple personalities—only after several of Milligan's selves read *Flowers for Algernon* and agreed to work with the author.

Now retired from Ohio University and living in Boca Raton, Florida, Keyes has recently completed a new novel and seen his work attain tremendous popularity in Japan. *Daniel Keyes Collected Stories* (1993) and *The Daniel Keyes Reader* (1994), and the sequel to *The Minds of Billy Milligan, The Milligan Wars* (1993), have all been published in Japan, with *The Milligan Wars* appearing in a U.S. edition in 1996.

Part I—Charlie Becomes a Genius

Flowers for Algernon is told as a series of "Progress Reports" written by Charlie Gordon, a thirty-two-year-old man with an IQ of 68. As Keyes's novel opens, Charlie has volunteered to be the subject of an experimental surgical procedure which would more than triple his IQ. Although Charlie is of subnormal intelligence, he is unusually motivated, taking night school classes at the Beekman University Center for Retarded Adults. At first, he is afraid he won't be chosen for the project. He doesn't understand what to do when he is asked to tell what he sees in inkblots, and when he traces through a diagram of a maze in competition with Algernon, a mouse who is running an actual maze, Algernon always wins. Nonetheless, Charlie is chosen by the scientists in charge of the project—Professor Nemur, the psychologist who developed the technique, and Dr. Strauss, the neurosurgeon who performs the actual operation.

After the surgery, Charlie returns to his job as a janitor at Donner's Bakery, where nobody is aware of his operation. The sad state of Charlie's life prior to the surgery is made clear when Joe Carp and Frank Reilly, whom Charlie regards as his friends, take him out to a bar, get him drunk, make fun of him, and leave him to find his way home.

As time passes, however, it becomes obvious that Charlie is getting smarter. At the bakery, he successfully operates a complicated machine that mixes baking dough. His performances on the psychological tests improve, and he finally beats Algernon at running the maze—a significant development, as the mouse has had its intelligence raised by the same surgical procedure that Charlie underwent. And his Progress Reports are more sophisticated and articulate than before.

As Charlie's IQ increases, so does his awareness of himself and others. Now, when his "friends" make fun of him, he understands their true motivations. He steadily advances at work, but takes no satisfaction from it because the other employees resent him. Eventually, his coworkers at the bakery are so unnerved by his unexplained changes that they sign a petition demanding that he be fired. The only one who doesn't, an old woman named Fanny Birden, nonetheless thinks Charlie's condition "ain't right" and wishes he could return to "the good simple man" he had been.

Charlie also realizes that he has fallen in love with Alice Kinnian, the night school teacher who originally recommended him for the operation. Despite the gentleness of her rejection, Charlie is terribly upset, as he is when he catches Gimpy, the one person at the bakery who had been kind to him, stealing. Charlie is becoming aware that factual knowledge and intellectual ability may not prepare a person to deal with all of life's problems.

Part 11—Charlie as a Genius

As Charlie tries to cram a lifetime of intellectual and emotional development into a period of months, he also increases his self-awareness by recovering lost memories, a process triggered by sleep-learning devices and continued through his ongoing psychotherapy sessions with Dr. Strauss. Through a series of flashbacks, we learn the agonizing details of Charlie's early life. Charlie's father, Matt, tried to do the best he could for his son. But Charlie's mother, Rose, denied that there was anything "wrong" with him and beat him when he was unable to learn like other children. However, when Charlie's sister Norma was born with normal intelligence, Rose turned against Charlie and sought to "protect" Norma from him, reacting with particular violence to anything he did that showed his developing sexuality. Finally, after an hysterical outburst in which Rose threatened to kill Charlie, Matt took Charlie to live with his uncle Herman. When Herman died several years later, Rose tried to have Charlie committed to the Warren State Home and Training School, an institution for the mentally handicapped, but Charlie avoided this when the owner of Donner's Bakery, a lifelong friend of his uncle Herman, offered him a job. The "new" Charlie now realizes that both his extraordinary motivation to learn and his confused responses to women are rooted in how he was treated by his mother.

As Charlie's IQ surges to nearly triple its original level, his relationship with Alice deepens, but when she is finally able to return his feelings, his childhood traumas leave him unable to make love to her. More importantly, the gap between their respective IQs makes it harder and harder for them to communicate, a problem the genius Charlie now has with almost everyone. In particular, he has come to regard Nemur and Strauss, who previously seemed unapproachable geniuses, as narrowlyfocused specialists more interested in acquiring fame and power than they are in increasing knowledge and helping others. When Nemur and Strauss take Charlie and Algernon to a psychologists' conference in Chicago to announce the success of their procedure, Charlie is outraged by their treating him like an object on display rather than as a human being. He is also disturbed by what appears to be an error in Nemur's analysis of the "waiting period" after the operation. Disgusted, Charlie deliberately lets Algernon loose in the conference room. While the others are frantically trying to recover the mouse, Charlie slips Algernon in his pocket, leaves the conference, and returns to New York, where he rents an apartment and drops out of sight.

Now completely on his own, Charlie devotes himself to reading, thinking, and recovering his memories. During this time he forms a relationship with Fay Lillman, a painter who lives down the hall. Charlie is attracted to Fay's free spirit and lack of inhibitions, but, as with Alice, he is unable to have a sexual relationship with her. His sense of isolation increases. Yearning for meaningful contact with others, he walks the streets of New York feeling an "unbearable hunger" for human contact. He even goes to visit his father, who left his mother several years earlier. His father fails to recognize him, and Charlie cannot bring himself to reveal his identity. A few days later, while dining alone in a restaurant, Charlie witnesses a young man drop a stack of dishes:

> When the owner came to see what the excitement was about, the boy cowered—threw up his arms as if to ward off a blow.
>
> "All right! All right, you dope," shouted the man, "don't just stand there! Get the broom and sweep up that mess. A broom … a broom! you idiot! It's in the kitchen. Sweep up all the pieces."
>
> When the boy saw that he was not going to be punished, his frightened expression disappeared, and he smiled and hummed as he came back with the broom. A few of the rowdier customers kept up the remarks, amusing themselves at his expense.
>
> "Here, sonny, over here. There's a nice piece behind you … "
>
> "C'mon, do it again …"
>
> "He's not so dumb. It's easier to break 'em than to wash 'em…."
>
> As the boy's vacant eyes moved

across the crowd of amused onlookers, he slowly mirrored their smiles and finally broke into an uncertain grin at the joke which he did not understand.

I felt sick inside as I looked at his dull, vacuous smile—the wide, bright eyes of a child, uncertain but eager to please, and I realized what I had recognized in him. They were laughing at him because he was retarded.

And at first I had been amused along with the rest.

Suddenly, I was furious at myself and all those who were smirking at him. I wanted to pick up the dishes and throw them. I wanted to smash their laughing faces. I jumped up and shouted: "Shut up! Leave him alone! He can't understand. He can't help what he is … but for God's sake, have some respect! *He's a human being!*"

The incident makes Charlie decide to return to Beekman University and work on his own to perfect Nemur and Strauss's procedure so that it might help others like himself.

After returning to the University, Charlie renews his relationship with Alice but is still unable to make love to her. He turns back to Fay, whom he does not truly love but with whom he is able, finally, to have a sexual relationship. Eventually, though, Charlie becomes so immersed in his research that he moves into the lab and breaks off with Fay, who resents the time he devotes to his work—and who also has never known the truth about Charlie. Time is of the essence, as Algernon is beginning to show signs of instability and decline. Charlie works feverishly to determine if the effects of his operation will last, driven both by his fear of reverting to his former self and his desire to find any information at all that might help other mentally handicapped people. He also begins to achieve a more mature insight into his own nature and that of other people. In a confrontation with Nemur, Charlie declares that "intelligence and education that hasn't been tempered by human affection isn't worth a damn."

Part III—Charlie Loses His Genius

Finally, Charlie's completes his research. In a letter to Nemur, he announces his discovery of the "Algemon-Gordon Effect": "artificially-induced intelligence deteriorates at a rate of time directly proportional to the quantity of the increase." Charlie will revert to his former IQ within a matter of months. Shortly after this discovery, Algernon dies.

Faced with the prospect of losing all he has gained, Charlie seeks to come to terms with himself and his memories. He visits his mother and sister, who still live in Brooklyn. Rose has sunk into senility and only momentarily recognizes her son. Norma, far from being the hateful rival Charlie remembers, is a kind and intelligent woman who sincerely regrets both Charlie's hardships and her own inability to help him through them.

Charlie also comes to terms with Alice Kinnian, who is determined to stick by him as long as possible. Having put the ghosts of his past to rest, he is finally able to make love to her, and they are fully together for a brief time. But Charlie's decline is rapid, and he pushes Alice away before he completely reverts to his former self.

Charlie's final Progress Reports reflect his rapid deterioration as his writing reverts to its earlier semi-literacy. However, he has retained some memory of his experiences, and perhaps some insight as well. When he goes back to his old job at the bakery, he notes, "if they make fun of you dont get sore because you remember their not so smart like you once thot they were." The bakery workers accept him back; Carp and Reilly, who formerly had tormented Charlie, defend him when a new worker makes fun of him. However, Charlie finally decides to leave New York for good and check himself into the Warren State Home and Training School. His final Progress Report, dated only eight months after the first, asks that someone "put some flowrs on Algernons grave in the bak yard."

Characters

Algernon

The mouse who was the first subject of the surgery which raised Charlie's intelligence. Charlie forms a close emotional bond with the mouse, who is the only other creature to have had its intelligence artificially raised. Its experiences, and fate, parallel Charlie's.

Fanny Birden

An older woman who works at the bakery with Charlie and who is the only employee who does not sign a petition demanding Charlie's resignation after his IQ is raised. She compares the change in Charlie's intelligence to Adam and Eve eating of the fruit of the Tree of Knowledge and wishes that Charlie "could go back to being the good simple man you was before."

Joe Carp

One of Charlie's coworkers at the bakery, and, with Frank Reilly, one of his chief tormentors.

Mr. Arthur Donner

The owner of the bakery where Charlie works,

Mr. Donner is a friend of Charlie's Uncle Herman and gave Charlie his job there. Unlike many others at the bakery, he treats Charlie decently, if condescendingly.

Gimpy

A worker at Donner's bakery who treats Charlie better than many of the other workers do. However, Gimpy is the cause of one of the postoperative Charlie's first major crises when Charlie sees him stealing from the cash register. When Charlie confronts him about stealing, Gimpy says, "I always stood up for you. I should of had my head examined."

Charlie Gordon

The narrator and central character of *Flowers for Algernon,* Charlie Gordon is a 32-year-old man with an IQ of 68. As a child, Charlie had a father who loved him and tried to take care of him, but he was abused by his mother, an emotionally unstable woman. His mother at first refused to admit that there was anything "wrong" with Charlie and beat him when he did not perform up to the standards of other children. When Charlie's sister was born with normal intelligence, his mother admitted his handicap but became obsessed with the fear that Charlie would harm his sister—especially, that he would sexually molest her. This unreasoning fear led Charlie's mother to violently repress any display of sexuality on Charlie's part and, eventually, to threaten to kill him if he was not removed from their home.

This pattern of childhood abuse marked the adult Charlie in two significant ways: with repressed sexuality and with a strong desire to learn. It was the latter that led him to take night classes at the Beekman School and which led to his being accepted as a subject for an operation that would raise his intelligence. Before the operation, Charlie is perceived as a "good, simple man" and a "likeable, retarded young man." His main goal in undergoing the operation is "to be smart like other pepul so I can have lots of friends who like me."

However, once Charlie attains normal intelligence, he sees that many people he thought were his friends were actually ridiculing and abusing him, and once he attains a genius IQ, he finds himself as remote and alienated from other people as he had been previously. He struggles to deal with the emotions he now has the intellect to recognize, but which his intellect alone cannot control. He also works to recover and come to terms with memories of his childhood. Through it all, Charlie's main desire is what it always has been: to be treated as a human being and to be able to establish satisfactory relationships with other human beings.

Although Charlie demonstrates some character flaws after his intelligence peaks, such as arrogance and self-absorption, he is basically a good man. When he realizes that the surgical procedure is flawed, he throws himself into research to discover the flaw, feeling that if his efforts contribute at all to "the possibility of helping others like myself, I will be satisfied." When he finally determines that nothing can be done to prevent his return to his pre-operative state, he does what he can to come to terms with his family and those around him, and they in turn recognize his worth as a human being. Even after Charlie returns to his previous subnormal level of intelligence, he has learned to be understanding of the failings of others because they are "not so smart like you once thot they were." Although the experiment has failed, Charlie Gordon has not.

Matt Gordon

Charlie's father, a salesman of barbershop supplies. He is basically a kind man who loves his son and tries to protect him but who is consistently overpowered by his wife: first, by her hysterical denial that Charlie is handicapped, and then by her equally hysterical conviction that Charlie is a danger to their daughter. When Rose threatens to kill Charlie, Matt takes Charlie to his Uncle Herman, who offers Charlie a refuge. Years later, Matt finally leaves Rose and opens his own barbershop. When the adult Charlie seeks him out, he does not recognize his son.

Norma Gordon

Charlie's sister. Charlie's memory of her is of a "spoiled brat" who hated him and treated him badly.

However, when the adult Charlie visits the adult Norma, who now has full-time care of their senile mother, he finds a grown woman who is "warm and sympathetic and affectionate." She genuinely regrets her youthful hostility towards her brother, and wants to reestablish contact with him.

Rose Gordon

Charlie's mother. She is an emotionally unstable woman who was largely unable to cope with having a mentally handicapped child. During Charlie's early childhood, she refused to admit that he was anything other than "normal" and beat him when he was unable to perform at the same level as other children. After Charlie's sister Norma was born without mental handicaps, Rose quit trying to make Charlie "normal" and became obsessed with "protecting" Norma from him. Eventually, Rose breaks down completely, declares that Norma is in danger of being sexually molested by Charlie, and threatens to kill him if he is not removed from their home. When Charlie reestablishes contact with his mother many years later, he discovers an old woman far gone into senility who barely recognizes her son.

Media Adaptations

- The original short story version of *Flowers for Algernon* was adapted for television as *The Two Worlds of Charlie Gordon* for CBS Playhouse in 1961.

- The novel *Flowers for Algernon* was made into the feature film *Charly* in 1968. Cliff Robertson won the Academy Award as Best Actor for his portrayal of Charlie Gordon. Available from CBS/Fox Home Video.

- The novel has also been presented on the stage. David Rogers adapted the novel as a two-act play, *Flowers for Algernon*, in 1969; a dramatic musical, *Charlie and Algernon*, was first produced in Canada in 1978 and played on Broadway in 1980. Stage plays based on the novel have also been produced in France, Australia, Poland, and Japan.

- *Flowers for Algernon* has also been adapted for radio: as a monodrama for Irish radio in 1983, and as a radio play in Czechoslovakia in 1988.

Hilda

A nurse who attends Charlie immediately after the operation and who tells him that the scientists should not have altered his intelligence. She compares their action to Adam and Eve eating the fruit of the Tree of Knowledge and being cast out of Eden.

Miss Alice Kinnian

Charlie Gordon's teacher at the Beekman University Center for Retarded Adults, the person who recommends Charlie for the procedure which raises his intelligence, and the woman Charlie loves. Alice is an intelligent and dedicated woman who takes a strong personal interest in Charlie and consistently treats him in a responsible and respectful manner. As Charlie's intelligence increases, she guides him as best she can; when he falls in love with her, she gently declines. However, they maintain a close friendship, and Alice eventually finds herself returning Charlie's feelings, only to discover that the traumas of his past prevent him from making love to her. She remains his friend, despite the increasing distance his towering intelligence places between them. When the operation finally fails and Charlie enters his decline, they are finally able to have a romantic relationship. Alice tries her best to stick by Charlie, even when he pushes her away, but when he is finally back where he began, with an IQ of 68, she is forced to admit that he is lost to her and that she has to go on with her life.

Fay Lillman

A free-spirited artist who lives across the hall from Charlie when he "disappears" in New York. When Charlie first sees her painting in her underwear, she thinks nothing of it, and she does not hesitate to crawl along a window ledge to get to Charlie's apartment. Charlie eventually enters into a sexual relationship with her, although he does not love her, and she provides Charlie with a whirlwind social life of drinking, dancing, and having a good time. Although she evidently feels genuine affection for Charlie, she is uninterested in his research, perhaps in part because she does not know that Charlie has had his intelligence artificially raised. When Charlie moves into the lab because Fay is interfering with his work, she loses interest in him and drifts away.

Bertha Nemur

Professor Harold Nemur's wife. An ambitious woman who used her father's influence to get Professor Nemur the grant that funded his research and who is constantly pressuring her husband to excel and produce great results. According to Burt Selden, she is why Nemur is "under tension all the time, even when things are going well...."

Professor Harold Nemur

The psychologist who developed the theories behind the operation which raised Charlie's intelligence. Nemur is a brilliant scientist but egotistical and ambitious, the latter stemming partially from pressures from his wife. He is eager to establish his reputation as the discoverer of the process that made Charlie a genius and rushes to make the results of the experiment public, against the advice of the other scientists working on the project. He does not initially want Charlie to be the subject of the experiment, and after Charlie's IQ is raised, relations between the two are often strained, as Charlie's intelligence eventually exceeds Nemur's. This hostility culminates in a shouting match between the two during which Charlie accuses Nemur of treating him as less than a human being and Nemur accuses Charlie of having become "arrogant, self-centered," and "antisocial."

Frank Reilly

One of Charlie's coworkers at the bakery, and, with Joe Carp, one of his chief tormentors.

Burt Seldon

A graduate student who assists Professor Nemur and Dr. Strauss. He is in charge of Charlie's psychological testing, and he treats Charlie in a more relaxed and friendly fashion than either of the senior scientists. It is through Burt that Charlie gets much of his information about Nemur and Strauss, and it is Burt who suggests that the post-operative Charlie needs to develop "understanding" and "tolerance."

Dr. Strauss

Dr. Strauss, Professor Nemur's partner, is the neurosurgeon who performs the surgery that raises Charlie's IQ. He is more sympathetic to and concerned for Charlie than is Nemur. He advocates that Charlie be chosen for the experiment, intervenes when Charlie has a potentially violent confrontation with Nemur, and tries to look after Charlie when the effects of the experiment have finally worn off.

Thelma

A nurse at the Warren State Home who impresses Charlie by her devotion to her patients. Because he already knows he is regressing and could end up as a resident of Warren, Charlie

wonders what it would be like to have her care for
him.

Science and Technology

Relating the story of a mentally impaired man whose intelligence is increased through surgery and then lost, *Flowers for Algernon* touches on a number of literary themes. The most obvious of the novel's themes is the use and abuse of science and technology. The critic Mark R. Hillegas has identified *Flowers for Algernon* as the type of science fiction which deals with "problems imagined as resulting from inventions, discoveries, or scientific hypotheses"—in this case, a surgical procedure that can turn a person of subnormal intelligence into a genius. While the novel does not specifically take an anti-technology stance, it does make clear the limitations of technology as a "quick fix" to human problems—Charlie's operation is, ultimately, a failure in that he does not remain a genius. In a reversal of the classic notion of tragedy, the "flaw" which causes Charlie's downfall is not within him, but in the technology which sought to change him.

Knowledge and Ignorance

The idea that "there are some things humanity was not meant to know" may be traced in modern literature to Mary Shelley's novel *Frankenstein* (1818), and in some ways *Flowers for Algernon* contains echoes of Shelley's tale. The critic Thomas D. Clareson has directly connected Keyes's novel to *Frankenstein* in that Keyes combines the figures of the mad scientist and the "inhuman" creation into "the single figure of Charlie Gordon." This theme is further emphasized by the comments of Hilda, a nurse, and Fanny Birden, one of Charlie's coworkers, which compare his operation to the acquisition of forbidden knowledge in the Garden of Eden, which resulted in Adam and Eve being thrown out of Paradise.

However, *Flowers for Algernon* does not argue that humans should not try to attain knowledge, but rather that they should be conscious of the limitations of a purely intellectual approach to life. When Charlie buries himself in research to try to find the solution to the flaw in the operation, he declares, "I'm living at a peak of clarity and beauty I never knew existed." But later, during an argument with Professor Nemur, Charlie acknowledges that intelligence alone isn't enough: "intelligence and education isn't worth a damn … all too often a search for knowledge drives out the search for love."

Topics for Further Study

- Research the history of public attitudes towards mental retardation in the United States and discuss the problems Charlie Gordon faces in the novel in the context of this history.

- Research Sigmund Freud's theories of psychology and discuss how Charlie Gordon's emotional problems *(not* his low IQ) can be explained in terms of Freudian analysis.

- Read the original short story version of *Flowers for Algernon* and compare it with the novel. What changes have been made, and how do those changes affect the reader's response to the story?

Alienation and Loneliness

In an early "progress report," Charlie writes that he wants to be smart "so I can have lots of friends who like me." Unfortunately, once he becomes a genius, he discovers that there are a whole new set of problems that prevent him from establishing satisfactory relationships with other people. He has substituted one sort of alienation for another, as the condescension and cruelty he once faced from humanity has been replaced by misunderstanding, insensitivity, and fear. He falls in love with Alice Kinnian, the teacher who recommended him for the operation, but he realizes, "I am just as far away from Alice with an I.Q. of 185 as I was when I had an I.Q. of 70." Almost everything Charlie does in the novel is motivated by his desire to understand himself and establish functional relationships with others, perhaps most dramatically expressed when he wanders the streets of New York City by himself: "for a moment I brush against someone and sense the connection."

Atonement and Forgiveness

A major aspect of the novel is Charlie's efforts to understand and come to terms with the various people who have hurt him throughout his life: his mother, who physically and emotionally abused him; his father, who failed to defend him; his coworkers at the bakery, who brutalized him; the scientists who raised his intelligence but treated him like a laboratory animal. It is significant that when Charlie realizes the effects of the operation will not last, his major goal is to locate his family and establish some sort of peace with them. When he finally locates his mother, he tells himself, "I must understand the way she saw it. Unless I forgive her, I will have nothing." The tragedy of Charlie's fall from genius is relieved somewhat by the knowledge that he has come to terms with the people who mistreated him. In his last progress report, he writes, "if they make fun of you dont get sore because you remember their not so smart like you once thot they were."

Prejudice and Tolerance

Written during the height of the civil rights movement in the United States, *Flowers for Algernon* shows a profound concern with the rights of individuals to be treated as individuals, no matter what their condition in life. The early pages of the novel paint a grim portrait of how the mentally handicapped are treated, as Charlie is continually abused, verbally and physically, by his coworkers at the bakery. And when he becomes a genius, he is subject to a different sort of dehumanization, as the scientists in charge of the experiment regard him "as if I were some kind of newly created thing.... No one ... considered me an individual— a human being." This is perhaps most dramatically expressed when, witnessing a slow-witted boy being ridiculed for breaking dishes in a restaurant, Charlie lashes out at the customers: "Leave him alone! He can't understand. He can't help what he is ... but for God's sake, have some respect! *He's a human being!"*

Sex

Although the novel is not primarily focused on sexual issues, a good deal of attention is paid to the fact that Charlie is sexually repressed as a result of an abused childhood. His mother, terrified that her "retarded" son would sexually assault his "normal" sister, violently repressed all normal displays of adolescent sexuality. The adult Charlie, once his intelligence has been raised to where he can understand the issues involved, initially has difficulty establishing a sexual relationship with Fay Lillman, a neighbor who seeks out his company, and is unable to have a physical relationship with Alice Kinnian, the woman he is in love with. Charlie's ability to have sex with Fay and, eventually, with Alice, is seen as an important step in overcoming past traumas and becoming a fully functional adult.

Point of View

Keyes's remarkable use of first-person ("I") point of view is perhaps the most important source of *Flowers for Algernon's* narrative power. Charlie's journey from an IQ of 68 to one almost three times as high, and his fall back into subnormal intelligence, is told in the form of "Progress Reports" written by Charlie for the scientists conducting the experiment that raised his IQ. The reports before and soon after the operation are written in nonstandard English, full of the kind of mistakes one would expect from writing by a mentally handicapped adult:

> Dr Strauss says I shoud rite down what I think and remembir and evrey thing that happins to me from now on. I dont no why but he says its importint so they will see if they can use me.

As Charlie's intelligence grows, his reports become more and more literate and sophisticated:

> I've got to realize that when they continually admonish me to speak and write simply so that people who read these reports will be able to understand me, they are talking

about themselves as well.

The striking contrasts between the earlier and later entries, both in style and content, dramatize both the changes Charlie undergoes and the obstacles he must overcome. Even more dramatic is the contrast between the high-IQ entries and the final entries, when Charlie loses his intelligence and falls back into the semi-literacy of the earlier entries. Keyes's use of Charlie as the narrator makes the reader's experience of Charlie's inevitable fate more immediate and more moving, and shows that, as a reviewer in the *Times Literary Supplement* put it, Keyes "has the technical equipment to keep us from shrugging off the pain."

Foreshadowing

Another source of the novel's power is the inevitability of Charlie's fate, once we learn that the results of the experiment will not be permanent. But even before we learn that the experiment has failed, Keyes offers several moments of foreshadowing, events which hint at what is to come. The most obvious of these center around Algernon the mouse, who has had the same operation as Charlie and whose progress and deterioration both mirrors and forecasts Charlie's own. When Algernon begins to grow restive, has trouble running the maze, and starts biting people, it does not bode well for Charlie. In addition, two minor characters—Hilda, a nurse, and Fanny Birden, one of Charlie's coworkers at the bakery—both invoke the story of

Adam and Eve's expulsion from the Garden of Eden, which foreshadows Charlie's own "fall" from genius. Charlie's trip to the Warren State Home while he still possesses heightened intelligence foreshadows what is in store when he finally loses that intelligence. And, in a more subtle moment early in the novel, as Charlie is on the operating table before the surgery, he tells Dr. Strauss that he's scared. When Dr. Strauss reassures him that he will "just go to sleep," Charlie replies, "thats what I'm skared about"—a foreshadowing, perhaps, of Charlie's later descent into darkness.

Setting

The setting of *Flowers for Algernon* is New York City, with a brief episode in Chicago, in the present or near future. Although the physical landscape and cultural background is not a major part of the novel, critic Robert Scholes has noted that the very normality and non-distinctiveness of the setting makes the one "different" element of the novel—the surgical procedure that raises Charlie's IQ—all the more distinctive. And at one point in the novel, when Charlie has taken Algernon and is hiding out from the scientists, the crowded urban landscape of New York City becomes an important part of Charlie's attempts to come to terms with his situation: "on a hot night when everyone is out walking, or sitting in a theater, there is a rustling, and for a moment I brush against someone and sense the connection between the branch and trunk and the deep root."

Irony

Irony—the difference between the way things appear to be and the way they really are—plays an important part in *Flowers for Algernon*. Early in the novel, we see that Charlie's coworkers at the bakery, especially Joe Carp and Frank Reilly, are condescending and abusive towards him, insulting him to his face and playing cruel tricks on him. Charlie, however, writes that "Lots of people laff at me and their my friends and we have fun.... I cant wait to be smart like my best friends Joe Carp and Frank Reilly." Once Charlie becomes smart, he realizes that these people are not his friends, but he is then faced with another irony. Before the operation, he wanted "to be smart like other pepul so I can have lots of frends who like me." But his increased IQ causes the bakery workers to be afraid of him, the scientists who had been kindly and wise figures turn out to be limited human beings who see Charlie more as a laboratory experiment than a human being, and heightened intelligence is no help when he falls in love with Alice Kinnian. As Charlie the genius notes, "Ironic that all my intelligence doesn't help me solve a problem like this." And in a final irony, when Charlie returns to his IQ of 68 and seeks his old job back, Joe and Frank, the men who had persecuted him before, defend him against an attack from a new worker.

Tragedy

In literature, tragedy refers to works where a

person, often of great achievement, is destroyed through a character flaw that he or she possesses. In classic tragedy, this "fall" is often from a great height (Oedipus and Hamlet were both royalty, for example) and is inevitable, given the character's character flaw. *Flowers for Algernon* is certainly about a fall from a height, and Charlie's descent from genius to subnormal intelligence is inevitable. Charlie does have character flaws—an arrogance and impatience which appear when he becomes a genius— but these do not lead to his fall. Instead, the "flaw" is outside of Charlie, in the technology which raises him to a great height and then allows him to fall back down. In this way, Keyes is able to use the devices of tragedy to make a very modern point: that our technology is as imperfect as we are.

Civil Rights in the 1960s

The issue which lies at the heart of *Flowers for Algernon* is Charlie Gordon's struggle to be recognized and treated as a human being. Prior to his operation, he was regarded as somehow less than fully human because of his subnormal intelligence. After the operation, he is discriminated against in a different way, as ordinary people shun him and the scientists who raised his IQ treat him as little more than another laboratory specimen. It should come as no surprise that this story of a person who manages to be a member of two different minorities—the mentally handicapped and the mentally superior—should have appeared during a time of growing awareness of the problems and the rights of minority groups.

The period from the first publication of *Flowers for Algernon* as a short story to its publication as a novel, the period from 1959 to 1966, saw the rise of the civil rights movement in the United States. Although most immediately and dramatically focused on the task of securing equal rights for African Americans, the civil rights movement was accompanied by increasing attention to the issue of fair and equal treatment for all. The 1964 Civil Rights Bill prohibited racial discrimination; 1966, the year *Flowers for Algernon* was published, saw the founding of the National Organization for Women. The rights of the mentally handicapped were also addressed during this time: in 1962 the President's Panel on Mental Retardation was organized, leading in 1968 to the Declaration of the General and Specific Rights of the Mentally Retarded. By the 1970s, the term "retardation" was replaced with "developmental disability," and specific provisions for the protection of the mentally handicapped from violence and discrimination became law. *Flowers for Algernon's* message of tolerance and understanding for the mentally handicapped reflects the social and political struggles of its day, and the years following the novel's publication saw many of these issues regarding developmental disability finally addressed in the legislature and the courts.

Compare & Contrast

- **1960s:** The civil rights movement was in full force, with passage of legislation addressing discrimination against African Americans and increasing awareness of the rights of other oppressed groups, including the mentally handicapped. However, prejudice was still widespread, and there was as yet little to no legal protection for mentally handicapped persons.

  Today: Legislative and legal

protection for the mentally handicapped is extensive, while public sensitivity to the rights of the handicapped has increased markedly. Terms such as "retarded" and "feeble-minded" have been replaced with less negatively-charged terms such as "mentally challenged" and "developmentally disabled." However, civil rights as a whole is in a volatile period, as the public at large seems increasingly resistant to the demands of minority groups.

- **1960s:** Psychoanalysis is increasingly accepted as a means of dealing with mental illness, while the theories of Sigmund Freud enjoy widespread public awareness and acceptance.

Today: The treatment of emotional disorders is increasingly diverse, with traditional psychoanalysis complemented by various holistic, Eastern, and "New Age" approaches, as well as by the development of increasingly effective antidepressants and other psychoactive drugs. However, the theories of Sigmund Freud are not as widely accepted as in the past, and the public at large appears impatient with what it sees as abnormal or dangerous behavior "excused" because of past trauma.

- **1960s:** The pressures of the Cold War lead to an unprecedented amount of spending on scientific research by both the U.S. government and private foundations and corporations.

  Today: With the Cold War over and budgets shrinking, competition for research funding is more intense than ever, and funding agencies are increasingly reluctant to support research that does not have immediate, practical results.

Psychology and the Rise of Scientific Research

In addition to the Civil Rights movement, the 1950s and 1960s also saw the rise of psychoanalysis as a generally accepted method of dealing with emotional disorders. The theories of Sigmund Freud, which saw human motivation as stemming largely from unconscious desires which are often traceable to childhood experiences and which frequently center on sex, were particularly influential during this time. Freud's theories were so widely discussed that most people, even if they were not trained in psychoanalysis, probably had some familiarity with concepts such as repression, neurosis, and the unconscious. Accordingly, the novel's focus on psychological themes, especially Charlie's emotional problems stemming from the abuse he suffered from his mother, was immediately familiar to the readers of the 1960s.

Also on the rise in the 1950s and 1960s was funding for scientific research. Locked in a Cold War with the Soviet Union and still remembering Nazi Germany's V-2 rockets and the terrifying success of the atomic bomb, the United States during this era spent an unprecedented amount of money on scientific research. Government organizations such as the National Science Foundation, as well as private foundations and corporations, poured millions of dollars into scientific research. This included "basic" research that would not necessarily yield immediate practical applications. With so much money available, competition for funding intensified and universities became increasingly focused on obtaining and keeping research funding. In *Flowers for Algernon*, Professor Nemur and Dr. Strauss's funding from the "Welburg Foundation," as well as the pressure Nemur feels to publish his results and secure his professional reputation, directly reflect this trend.

Critical Overview

There is not as much critical commentary on *Flowers for Algernon* as there is on some other contemporary novels. What criticism does exist has occasionally found fault with the novel on the grounds of sentimentality or predictability, but on the whole the critical response has been favorable. Critics have also noted the novel's status as a work of science fiction.

Typical of the critical response to Keyes's novel is Mark R. Hillegas' 1966 *Saturday Review* essay, which ranks *Flowers for Algernon* with Kurt Vonnegut's *Player Piano* and Walter M. Miller, Jr.'s *A Canticle for Leibowitz* as a "work of quality science fiction," although Hillegas finds the novel "considerably less powerful" than Vonnegut's or Miller's novels. Hillegas also notes that Keyes's novel is occasionally "marred by a cliched dialogue or a too predictable description." Nonetheless, he finds that the novel "offers compassionate insight into the situation of the mentally retarded" and is "profoundly moving."

Other contemporary reviews sounded much the same note. Eliot Fremont-Smith, writing in the *New York Times* in 1966, states that Keyes "has taken the obvious, treated it in a most obvious fashion, and succeeded in creating a tale that is convincing, suspenseful, and touching—all in modest degree, but it is enough." Despite the many potential problems, such as how to convincingly show Charlie as a genius, "the skill shown here is awesome," and "affecting, too—how otherwise explain the tears that come to one's eyes at the novel's end?" Similarly, a reviewer in the *Times Literary Supplement* finds some of the minor characters "less successfully created" but praises the novel as "a far more intelligent book than the vast majority of 'straight' novels."

What critical attention *Flowers from Algernon* has received since its original publication has come mostly from scholars discussing the novel as a work of science fiction. In his 1975 book *Structural Fabulation: An Essay on Fiction of the Future*, Robert Scholes discusses the novel as "minimal SF" that, unlike some works of science fiction, "establishes only one discontinuity between its world and our own"—in other words, the experiment which raises Charlie's intelligence. Scholes finds the novel "beautifully problematic" and asserts that its power derives largely from the fact that the results of the operation are impermanent. While "Keyes has fleshed out his idea with great skill," Scholes also sees the novel as "deficient in artistic integrity" because of its existence as both a short story and a novel.

More recently, the noted British SF writer and critic Brian W. Aldiss, in his 1986 book *Trillion Year Spree: The History of Science Fiction*, compares Charlie to the character of Lenny in John Steinbeck's *Of Mice and Men*. Unlike other critics, Aldiss prefers the original short story to the novel:

"This moving story lost something of its power when expanded to novel length." And in his 1990 study *Understanding Contemporary American Science Fiction*, Thomas D. Clareson claims that Keyes "revitalized the myth of Frankenstein by introducing a fresh narrative perspective" and combining "Mary Shelley's nameless creature and the crazed scientist into the single figure of Charlie." Clareson further notes that the novel's "narrative perspective" makes it "unique in the science fiction pantheon."

Sources

Brian W. Aldiss, with David Wingrove, in *Trillion Year Spree: The History of Science Fiction*, Gollancz, 1986.

Thomas D. Clareson, *Understanding Contemporary American Science Fiction: The Formative Period, 1926-1970*, University of South Carolina Press, 1990, pp. 231-33.

Eliot Fremont-Smith, "The Message and the Maze," in *New York Times*, March 7, 1966, p. 25.

Mark R. Hillegas, "Other Worlds to Conquer," in *Saturday Review*, Vol. 49, March 26, 1966, pp. 33-4.

"Making up a Mind" (review of *Flowers for Algernon*), in *Times Literary Supplement*, No. 3360, July 21, 1966, p. 629.

Robert Scholes, "Structural Fabulation," in his *Structural Fabulation: An Essay on Fiction of the Future*, University of Notre Dame Press, 1975, pp. 45-76.

For Further Study

DISCovering Most-Studied Authors, Gale, 1996.

Offers biographical and critical information about Keyes.

CPSIA information can be obtained
at www.ICGtesting.com
Printed in the USA
BVHW041721020721
611060BV00013B/1593

9 781375 398824